THE COMPLETE
EXCEL USER
GUIDE BOOK

**The Step-by-Step tutorials to Learning
all Essential Functions, and Master
Microsoft Excel from scratch**

Kane Schiller

Copyright

Table of Contents

Introduction

In a bustling city where every click of a keyboard and tap of a touchscreen echoed with ambition, there lived a young professional named Maya. Maya was bright and eager, with a hunger to excel in her career as a financial analyst. However, she found herself constantly struggling to keep up with the fast-paced demands of her job.

One day, while browsing through a bookstore during her lunch break, Maya stumbled upon a book titled "The Complete Excel User Guide Book." Intrigued by the promise of unlocking the secrets of Excel, Maya decided to purchase the book.

That evening, nestled in the comfort of her cozy apartment, Maya delved into the pages of the book. From the basics of spreadsheet navigation to the intricacies of advanced functions, Maya absorbed every word with rapt attention. She spent countless hours practicing the exercises, experimenting with formulas, and honing her skills with each chapter.

As weeks turned into months, Maya's proficiency in Excel began to soar. She effortlessly tackled complex financial models, streamlined data analysis processes, and impressed her colleagues with her newfound expertise. With each success, Maya's confidence grew, propelling her career to new heights.

Soon, Maya became the go-to person for Excel-related queries in her office. Colleagues sought her advice, managers relied on her insights, and clients marveled at her ability to transform raw data into actionable insights. Maya's reputation as an Excel wizard spread far and wide, earning her accolades and opportunities she had never imagined.

But Maya's journey didn't end there. Fueled by her passion for continuous learning, she delved deeper into Excel's vast universe, exploring advanced techniques, mastering specialized functions, and even dabbling in programming with Visual Basic for Applications (VBA). With each new skill acquired, Maya pushed the boundaries of what was possible with Excel, cementing her status as a true expert in the field.

Years later, as Maya reflected on her journey, she realized that the humble "Complete Excel User Guide Book" had been the catalyst for her transformation. It had not only equipped her with the technical know-how to excel in her career but had also instilled in her a sense of curiosity, perseverance, and determination to pursue excellence in everything she did.

And so, armed with her trusty book and an unwavering passion for learning, Maya continued to chart her course through the ever-changing landscape of Excel, knowing that the possibilities were limitless for those who dared to dream and dared to excel.

Chapter 1: Getting Started with Excel

Microsoft Excel is a powerful spreadsheet application used for data management, analysis, and visualization. Whether you're managing budgets, tracking progress, or analyzing large datasets, Excel's robust features make it an essential tool for professionals and beginners alike. In this chapter, we'll cover the basics to get you up and running with Excel, ensuring you have a solid foundation to build upon as you progress through this book.

Navigating the Excel Interface

Before diving into the functionalities of Excel, it's important to familiarize yourself with its interface.

Here's an overview of the main components you'll encounter:

- **Ribbon:** The Ribbon is the toolbar at the top of the Excel window, divided into tabs such as Home, Insert, Page Layout, Formulas, Data, Review, and View. Each tab contains groups of related commands.

- **Workbook:** A workbook is an Excel file that contains one or more worksheets. Each workbook can hold a vast amount of data organized in a structured manner.

- **Worksheet:** Also known as a spreadsheet, a worksheet is a single page within a workbook, made up of cells arranged in rows and columns.

- **Cells:** Cells are the basic units where you input data, identified by their column letter and row number (e.g., A1, B2).

- **Formula Bar:** Located above the worksheet, the Formula Bar displays the contents of the active cell and allows you to enter or edit data and formulas.

- Status Bar: Found at the bottom of the Excel window, the Status Bar provides information about the current state of your worksheet, including the sum, average, and count of selected cells.

- Quick Access Toolbar: A customizable toolbar that provides quick access to commonly used commands, such as Save, Undo, and Redo.

Basic Excel Functions and Formulas

Functions and formulas are the heart of Excel, allowing you to perform calculations and analyze data efficiently.

Here are some basic functions to get you started:

- SUM: Adds a range of cells. For example, `=SUM(A1:A5)` calculates the total of cells A1 through A5.

- **AVERAGE:** Calculates the average value of a range of cells. For example, `=AVERAGE(B1:B5)` returns the average of cells B1 through B5.

- **MIN and MAX:** Find the smallest and largest values in a range, respectively. For example, `=MIN(C1:C5)` and `=MAX(C1:C5)`.

- **COUNT:** Counts the number of cells in a range that contain numbers. For example, `=COUNT(D1:D5)`.

- **IF:** A logical function that returns one value if a condition is true and another value if it is false. For example, `=IF(E1>50, "Pass", "Fail")`.

Creating and Managing Worksheets

Creating and organizing worksheets efficiently is crucial for effective data management.

How to get started:

- Creating a New Workbook: Open Excel and select "New" to create a new workbook. Choose a blank workbook or a template that suits your needs.

- Adding Worksheets: To add a new worksheet, click the "+" icon next to the existing sheet tabs at the bottom of the screen.

- Renaming Worksheets: Double-click the sheet tab and type the new name. Press Enter to save the name.

- Deleting Worksheets: Right-click the sheet tab you want to delete and select "Delete." Confirm the action if prompted.

- Moving and Copying Worksheets: Drag the sheet tab to reorder it within the workbook. To copy, right-click the tab, select "Move or Copy," choose the destination, and check "Create a copy."

Customizing Excel Settings

Customizing Excel to suit your preferences can enhance your efficiency and comfort while working.

Here are some key settings you might want to adjust:

- **Default Font and Size:** Change the default font and size for new workbooks under File > Options > General.

- **Theme and Colors:** Customize the Excel theme and color scheme via File > Options > General > Office Theme.

- **Save Options:** Adjust the default save location and format under File > Options > Save. It's also wise to set up AutoSave and AutoRecover to prevent data loss.

- **Formula Settings:** Configure how Excel handles formulas, including enabling iterative calculations and adjusting the calculation mode (automatic or manual), under File > Options > Formulas.

- Language and Proofing: Set your preferred language and proofing options (such as spell check) via File > Options > Language.

By mastering these foundational skills and settings, you'll be well-prepared to dive deeper into Excel's more advanced features in the following chapters. Let's move forward and start mastering essential Excel functions that will transform the way you work with data.

Chapter 2: Mastering Essential Excel Functions

Excel functions are powerful tools that allow you to perform a wide variety of calculations and data manipulations efficiently. In this chapter, we'll explore some of the most essential functions that form the backbone of everyday Excel usage. By mastering these functions, you'll be able to handle a range of tasks from simple arithmetic to complex data analysis.

Basic Arithmetic and Statistical Functions

Arithmetic and statistical functions are the foundation of Excel's computational capabilities.

Some key functions you should be familiar with:

SUM

The SUM function is used to add up a range of numbers. It's one of the most frequently used functions in Excel.

Example: `=SUM(A1:A10)`
This formula adds all the numbers in cells A1 through A10.

AVERAGE
The AVERAGE function calculates the mean of a set of numbers.

Example: `=AVERAGE(B1:B10)`
This formula returns the average value of the numbers in cells B1 through B10.

MIN and MAX
The MIN function finds the smallest number in a range, while the MAX function finds the largest.

Example: `=MIN(C1:C10)`
This formula returns the smallest number in cells C1 through C10.

Example: `=MAX(C1:C10)`

This formula returns the largest number in cells C1 through C10.

COUNT

The COUNT function counts the number of cells in a range that contain numbers.

Example: `=COUNT(D1:D10)`

This formula counts the number of cells in the range D1 through D10 that contain numeric values.

COUNTA

The COUNTA function counts the number of non-empty cells in a range.

Example: `=COUNTA(E1:E10)`

This formula counts the number of cells in the range E1 through E10 that are not empty, including those with text, numbers, or other data types.

ROUND, ROUNDUP, and ROUNDDOWN

These functions round numbers to a specified number of digits. ROUND rounds to the nearest value, ROUNDUP always rounds up, and ROUNDDOWN always rounds down.

Example: `=ROUND(F1, 2)`
This formula rounds the number in cell F1 to two decimal places.

Example: `=ROUNDUP(F1, 2)`
This formula rounds the number in cell F1 up to two decimal places.

Example: `=ROUNDDOWN(F1, 2)`
This formula rounds the number in cell F1 down to two decimal places.

Text and Data Manipulation

Excel is not just about numbers; it also offers powerful text manipulation functions that can help you manage and clean data effectively.

CONCATENATE and CONCAT

The CONCATENATE function (or the newer CONCAT function) combines text from multiple cells into one cell.

Example: `=CONCATENATE(A1, " ", B1)`
This formula combines the text in cells A1 and B1, separated by a space.

Example: `=CONCAT(A1, " ", B1)`
This formula achieves the same result as CONCATENATE but uses the newer function.

TEXTJOIN

The TEXTJOIN function is similar to CONCATENATE but allows you to specify a delimiter and ignore empty cells.

Example: `=TEXTJOIN(", ", TRUE, A1:A5)`
This formula joins the text in cells A1 through A5, separated by a comma and space, and ignores any empty cells.

LEFT, RIGHT, and MID

These functions extract specified numbers of characters from text strings.

Example: `=LEFT(C1, 5)`
This formula extracts the first five characters from the text in cell C1.

Example: `=RIGHT(C1, 3)`
This formula extracts the last three characters from the text in cell C1.

Example: `=MID(C1, 2, 4)`
This formula extracts four characters from the text in cell C1, starting from the second character.

LEN
The LEN function returns the length of a text string.

Example: `=LEN(D1)`
This formula returns the number of characters in the text in cell D1.

TRIM

The TRIM function removes extra spaces from text, leaving only single spaces between words.

Example: `=TRIM(E1)`
This formula removes any leading, trailing, and extra spaces from the text in cell E1.

UPPER, LOWER, and PROPER
These functions change the case of text. UPPER converts text to uppercase, LOWER to lowercase, and PROPER capitalizes the first letter of each word.

Example: `=UPPER(F1)`
This formula converts the text in cell F1 to uppercase.

Example: `=LOWER(F1)`
This formula converts the text in cell F1 to lowercase.

Example: `=PROPER(F1)`
This formula capitalizes the first letter of each word in the text in cell F1.

Date and Time Functions

Managing dates and times effectively is crucial for many tasks in Excel. Here are some essential functions for working with date and time data:

TODAY and NOW

The TODAY function returns the current date, while the NOW function returns the current date and time.

Example: `=TODAY()`
This formula returns the current date.

Example: `=NOW()`
This formula returns the current date and time.

DATE and TIME

The DATE function creates a date value from individual year, month, and day components, while the TIME function creates a time value from individual hour, minute, and second components.

Example: `=DATE(2024, 5, 30)`
This formula returns the date May 30, 2024.

Example: `=TIME(14, 30, 0)`
This formula returns the time 2:30 PM.

YEAR, MONTH, DAY, HOUR, MINUTE, and SECOND

These functions extract individual components from date and time values.

Example: `=YEAR(G1)`
This formula returns the year from the date in cell G1.

Example: `=MONTH(G1)`
This formula returns the month from the date in cell G1.

Example: `=DAY(G1)`
This formula returns the day from the date in cell G1.

Example: `=HOUR(H1)`

This formula returns the hour from the time in cell H1.

Example: `=MINUTE(H1)`
This formula returns the minute from the time in cell H1.

Example: `=SECOND(H1)`
This formula returns the second from the time in cell H1.

DATEDIF

The DATEDIF function calculates the difference between two dates in various units (days, months, years).

Example: `=DATEDIF(I1, I2, "D")`
This formula returns the number of days between the dates in cells I1 and I2.

Example: `=DATEDIF(I1, I2, "M")`
This formula returns the number of months between the dates in cells I1 and I2.

Example: `=DATEDIF(I1, I2, "Y")`

This formula returns the number of years between the dates in cells I1 and I2.

Logical Functions and Conditional Statements

Logical functions allow you to perform actions based on conditions, making your spreadsheets dynamic and responsive.

IF

The IF function returns one value if a condition is true and another value if it is false.

Example: `=IF(J1>50, "Pass", "Fail")`

This formula returns "Pass" if the value in cell J1 is greater than 50, and "Fail" otherwise.

AND, OR, and NOT

These functions allow you to combine multiple conditions.

Example: `=AND(K1>50, K2<100)`

This formula returns TRUE if both conditions are true: K1 is greater than 50 and K2 is less than 100.

Example: `=OR(L1="Yes", L2="No")`
This formula returns TRUE if either condition is true: L1 is "Yes" or L2 is "No."

Example: `=NOT(M1="Complete")`
This formula returns TRUE if the value in cell M1 is not "Complete."

IFERROR
The IFERROR function returns a specified value if a formula results in an error, and the formula's result if there is no error.

Example: `=IFERROR(N1/O1, "Error")`
This formula returns "Error" if dividing N1 by O1 results in an error (such as division by zero), and the result of N1/O1 otherwise.

Lookup and Reference Functions

Lookup and reference functions are essential for finding and retrieving data from large datasets efficiently.

VLOOKUP

The VLOOKUP function searches for a value in the first column of a table and returns a value in the same row from a specified column.

Example: `=VLOOKUP(P1, A1:D10, 3, FALSE)`
This formula searches for the value in cell P1 within the first column of the range A1:D10 and returns the value in the third column of the matching row. The FALSE argument indicates an exact match is required.

HLOOKUP

The HLOOKUP function searches for a value in the top row of a table and returns a value in the same column from a specified row.

Example: `=HLOOKUP(Q1, A1:D10, 3, FALSE)`
This formula searches for the value in cell Q1 within the top row of the range A1:D10 and returns the

value in the third row of the matching column. The FALSE argument indicates an exact match is required.

INDEX and MATCH
The INDEX and MATCH functions are often

Basic Arithmetic and Statistical Functions

Arithmetic and statistical functions are the cornerstone of Excel's functionality, empowering users to perform a wide array of calculations with ease and precision. Mastering these fundamental operations is essential for any Excel user, from beginners to seasoned professionals.

Let's delve into some of the essential arithmetic and statistical functions that form the bedrock of Excel's computational prowess:

SUM:

The SUM function is a powerhouse for adding up values in a range of cells. It's your go-to tool for totaling expenses, sales figures, or any other numerical data.

Example: `=SUM(A1:A10)`
This formula computes the sum of the values in cells A1 through A10.

AVERAGE:

The AVERAGE function calculates the average value of a range of cells, providing insight into the typical value within a dataset.

Example: `=AVERAGE(B1:B10)`
This formula computes the average of the values in cells B1 through B10.

MIN and MAX:

MIN and MAX functions identify the smallest and largest values in a dataset, respectively, aiding in understanding the range and extremities of your data.

Example: `=MIN(C1:C10)`
This formula finds the smallest value in cells C1 through C10.

Example: `=MAX(C1:C10)`
This formula finds the largest value in cells C1 through C10.

COUNT:
The COUNT function tallies the number of cells containing numerical data within a given range, facilitating quick assessments of dataset size.

Example: `=COUNT(D1:D10)`
This formula counts the number of cells in the range D1 through D10 containing numeric values.

COUNTA:
COUNTA extends beyond numerical data, counting all non-empty cells within a range, including text and other non-numeric entries.

Example: `=COUNTA(E1:E10)`

This formula counts all non-empty cells in the range E1 through E10.

ROUND, ROUNDUP, and ROUNDDOWN:
These functions are indispensable for adjusting precision in numerical data, rounding values to desired decimal places.

Example: `=ROUND(F1, 2)`
This formula rounds the value in cell F1 to two decimal places.

Example: `=ROUNDUP(F1, 2)`
This formula rounds up the value in cell F1 to two decimal places.

Example: `=ROUNDDOWN(F1, 2)`
This formula rounds down the value in cell F1 to two decimal places.

These fundamental arithmetic and statistical functions pave the way for robust data analysis and modeling within Excel. By mastering these tools, you'll be equipped to tackle a myriad of tasks with confidence and precision, from basic calculations to complex statistical analyses. Excel's versatility and efficiency await your command, empowering you to unlock insights and drive informed decision-making.

Text and Data Manipulation

In Excel, effective text and data manipulation are pivotal for organizing, analyzing, and presenting information efficiently. Whether you're merging text strings, extracting specific characters, or cleaning up data, Excel provides a plethora of functions to streamline these tasks.

Let's see some essential text and data manipulation functions that will enhance your Excel proficiency:

CONCATENATE and CONCAT:
These functions combine multiple text strings into a single string, facilitating the creation of customized labels, addresses, or any other concatenated data.

Example: `=CONCATENATE(A1, " ", B1)`

This formula combines the text in cells A1 and B1 with a space between them.

Example: `=CONCAT(A1, " ", B1)`
Similar to CONCATENATE, this formula concatenates text in cells A1 and B1, but using the CONCAT function.

TEXTJOIN:
TEXTJOIN merges text from multiple cells, with the flexibility to specify a delimiter and ignore empty cells, offering precise control over the output.

Example: `=TEXTJOIN(", ", TRUE, A1:A5)`
This formula joins the text in cells A1 through A5, separated by a comma and space, while ignoring any empty cells.

LEFT, RIGHT, and MID:
These functions extract specific portions of text from a cell, enabling you to isolate relevant information such as first names, last names, or substrings.

Example: `=LEFT(C1, 5)`
This formula extracts the first five characters from the text in cell C1.

Example: `=RIGHT(C1, 3)`
This formula extracts the last three characters from the text in cell C1.

Example: `=MID(C1, 2, 4)`
This formula extracts four characters from the text in cell C1, starting from the second character.

LEN:
The LEN function returns the length of a text string, aiding in assessing the size and scope of text data.

Example: `=LEN(D1)`
This formula returns the number of characters in the text in cell D1.

TRIM:
TRIM removes leading, trailing, and excessive spaces from text, ensuring clean and standardized data.

Example: `=TRIM(E1)`

This formula removes extra spaces from the text in cell E1.

UPPER, LOWER, and PROPER:

These functions manipulate the case of text, converting it to uppercase, lowercase, or proper case (capitalizing the first letter of each word).

Example: `=UPPER(F1)`

This formula converts the text in cell F1 to uppercase.

Example: `=LOWER(F1)`

This formula converts the text in cell F1 to lowercase.

Example: `=PROPER(F1)`

This formula capitalizes the first letter of each word in the text in cell F1.

These text and data manipulation functions empower you to transform raw data into actionable insights, enabling clearer communication and more effective analysis. By harnessing the power of these tools, you'll streamline your workflow, enhance data integrity, and unlock the full potential of your Excel capabilities.

Date and Time Functions

Date and Time Functions

In Excel, managing date and time data is essential for various tasks, including scheduling, tracking deadlines, and analyzing trends over time. Excel offers a robust suite of date and time functions to manipulate, calculate, and format temporal data effectively.

Let's talk about some essential date and time functions that will empower you to handle temporal information with precision and efficiency:

TODAY and NOW:

These functions provide real-time information about the current date and time, allowing you to incorporate dynamic timestamps into your spreadsheets.

Example: `=TODAY()`
This formula returns the current date.

Example: `=NOW()`
This formula returns the current date and time.

DATE and TIME:
DATE and TIME functions construct date and time values based on specified components, enabling you to create custom dates and times for analysis and reporting.

Example: `=DATE(2024, 5, 30)`
This formula constructs the date May 30, 2024.

Example: `=TIME(14, 30, 0)`
This formula constructs the time at 2:30 PM.

YEAR, MONTH, DAY, HOUR, MINUTE, and SECOND:
These functions extract individual components (such as year, month, day, etc.) from date and time values, facilitating detailed analysis and reporting.

Example: `=YEAR(G1)`
This formula extracts the year from the date in cell G1.

Example: `=MONTH(G1)`
This formula extracts the month from the date in cell G1.

Example: `=DAY(G1)`
This formula extracts the day from the date in cell G1.

Example: `=HOUR(H1)`
This formula extracts the hour from the time in cell H1.

Example: `=MINUTE(H1)`

This formula extracts the minute from the time in cell H1.

Example: `=SECOND(H1)`
This formula extracts the second from the time in cell H1.

DATEDIF:
The DATEDIF function calculates the difference between two dates in various units (days, months, years), facilitating time-based analysis and reporting.

Example: `=DATEDIF(I1, I2, "D")`
This formula returns the number of days between the dates in cells I1 and I2.

Example: `=DATEDIF(I1, I2, "M")`
This formula returns the number of months between the dates in cells I1 and I2.

Example: `=DATEDIF(I1, I2, "Y")`
This formula returns the number of years between the dates in cells I1 and I2.

These date and time functions empower you to handle temporal data effectively, enabling you to perform a wide range of analyses, calculations, and reporting tasks with precision and accuracy. By mastering these tools, you'll gain greater insights into temporal trends, streamline your workflow, and enhance the effectiveness of your Excel spreadsheets.

Logical Functions and Conditional Statements

In Excel, logical functions and conditional statements are indispensable tools for decision-making, data analysis, and automation. These functions allow you to evaluate conditions and perform actions based on the results, enabling dynamic and intelligent spreadsheet operations.

Some essential logical functions and conditional statements that will enhance your Excel proficiency:

IF:

The IF function is a versatile tool that evaluates a condition and returns one value if the condition is true and another value if it is false.

Example: `=IF(J1>50, "Pass", "Fail")`
This formula returns "Pass" if the value in cell J1 is greater than 50, and "Fail" otherwise.

AND, OR, and NOT:

These functions enable you to combine multiple conditions and perform logical operations.

Example: `=AND(K1>50, K2<100)`
This formula returns TRUE if both conditions are true: K1 is greater than 50 and K2 is less than 100.

Example: `=OR(L1="Yes", L2="No")`
This formula returns TRUE if either condition is true: L1 is "Yes" or L2 is "No."

Example: `=NOT(M1="Complete")`

This formula returns TRUE if the value in cell M1 is not "Complete."

IFERROR:
The IFERROR function handles errors that may occur in formulas, allowing you to specify a value or action if an error occurs.

Example: `=IFERROR(N1/O1, "Error")`
This formula returns "Error" if dividing N1 by O1 results in an error (such as division by zero), and the result of N1/O1 otherwise.

These logical functions and conditional statements empower you to create dynamic and responsive spreadsheets, enabling you to automate decision-making processes, perform complex analyses, and streamline data processing tasks. By mastering these tools, you'll enhance the efficiency, accuracy, and intelligence of your Excel workflow, unlocking new possibilities for data-driven insights and informed decision-making.

Lookup and Reference Functions

In Excel, lookup and reference functions play a crucial role in retrieving and organizing data efficiently. Whether you're searching for specific values, referencing data from other sheets, or performing advanced lookup operations, Excel provides a range of functions to meet your needs.

Let's explore some essential lookup and reference functions that will enhance your ability to manage and analyze data effectively:

VLOOKUP:
The VLOOKUP function searches for a value in the first column of a table and returns a value in the same row from a specified column, enabling quick and efficient data retrieval.

Example: `=VLOOKUP(P1, A1:D10, 3, FALSE)`
This formula searches for the value in cell P1 within the first column of the range A1:D10 and returns the value in the third column of the matching row.

The FALSE argument indicates an exact match is required.

HLOOKUP:

The HLOOKUP function searches for a value in the top row of a table and returns a value in the same column from a specified row, providing flexibility in horizontal data lookup operations.

Example: `=HLOOKUP(Q1, A1:D10, 3, FALSE)`
This formula searches for the value in cell Q1 within the top row of the range A1:D10 and returns the value in the third row of the matching column. The FALSE argument indicates an exact match is required.

INDEX and MATCH:

The INDEX and MATCH functions work together to perform more flexible and powerful lookup operations, allowing you to search for a value in a range and return a corresponding value from another column or row.

Example: `=INDEX(A1:D10, MATCH(R1, B1:B10, 0), 3)`

This formula searches for the value in cell R1 within the range B1:B10 and returns the value in the third column of the matching row in the range A1:D10.

CHOOSE:

The CHOOSE function selects a value from a list of values based on a specified index number, providing a simple yet effective way to perform conditional lookups.

Example: `=CHOOSE(S1, "Apple", "Banana", "Orange")`

This formula selects a value from the list based on the value in cell S1. If S1 is 1, "Apple" is returned; if S1 is 2, "Banana" is returned, and so on.

ADDRESS and INDIRECT:

The ADDRESS function returns a cell address as text, while the INDIRECT function converts text into a cell reference, allowing for dynamic referencing of cells based on text values.

Example: `=INDIRECT(ADDRESS(T1, U1))`
This formula constructs a cell reference based on the values in cells T1 and U1 and returns the value of the referenced cell.

These lookup and reference functions empower you to efficiently retrieve, organize, and analyze data within Excel, enabling you to build dynamic and interactive spreadsheets that adapt to changing data and requirements. By mastering these tools, you'll streamline your data management processes, enhance data integrity, and unlock new possibilities for data-driven insights and decision-making.

Chapter 3: Advanced Excel Techniques

Excel is a versatile tool that offers a wide range of advanced techniques to help you manipulate, analyze, and visualize data effectively. By mastering these techniques, you can unlock the full potential of Excel and take your data management skills to the next level.

Some advanced Excel techniques that will enhance your productivity and efficiency:

Data Analysis with Excel:
Excel provides powerful tools for data analysis, including pivot tables, data validation, and what-if analysis. Pivot tables allow you to summarize and analyze large datasets quickly, while data validation ensures data integrity by restricting the type of data that can be entered into a cell. What-if analysis allows you to explore different scenarios by changing input values and observing the impact on calculated results.

Pivot Tables and Pivot Charts:

Pivot tables are one of Excel's most powerful features for summarizing and analyzing large datasets. They allow you to rearrange and summarize data dynamically, making it easy to identify trends and patterns. Pivot charts further enhance data visualization by providing graphical representations of pivot table data, making it easier to understand and interpret complex datasets.

Advanced Charting Techniques:

Excel offers a variety of advanced charting techniques, including combination charts, trendlines, and sparklines. Combination charts allow you to display multiple data series on a single chart, making it easier to compare and analyze different datasets. Trendlines help you identify trends and patterns in your data, while sparklines provide compact, inline visualizations that can be embedded directly within cells.

Macros and VBA for Automation:

Excel's built-in programming language, Visual Basic for Applications (VBA), allows you to automate repetitive tasks and customize Excel's functionality to suit your needs. You can use macros to record and replay sequences of commands, or write VBA code to create custom functions, automate data processing tasks, and build interactive user interfaces.

Using Excel for Financial Modeling:
Excel is widely used for financial modeling, including budgeting, forecasting, and valuation. Advanced Excel users can leverage financial functions such as NPV, IRR, and XNPV to perform complex financial calculations, as well as scenario analysis and sensitivity analysis to evaluate the impact of different assumptions on financial outcomes.

By mastering these advanced Excel techniques, you can streamline your workflow, improve the accuracy and efficiency of your data analysis, and gain valuable insights from your data. Whether you're a business analyst, financial analyst, or data scientist, Excel's advanced features provide a powerful toolkit for manipulating, analyzing, and visualizing data in a variety of contexts.

Data Analysis with Excel

Excel is a powerful tool for data analysis, offering a range of features and functions to manipulate, summarize, and visualize data effectively. Whether you're working with small datasets or large volumes of data, Excel provides the flexibility and functionality to perform a wide variety of data analysis tasks.

Let's explore some key aspects of data analysis with Excel:

Data Import and Cleansing:
Excel allows you to import data from a variety of sources, including databases, text files, and web pages. Once imported, you can use Excel's data cleansing tools to remove duplicates, correct errors, and format data appropriately for analysis.

Data Manipulation and Transformation:

Excel offers a range of functions and tools for manipulating and transforming data, including sorting, filtering, and grouping. You can also use formulas and functions to perform calculations, create derived variables, and transform data into different formats.

Pivot Tables and Pivot Charts:

Pivot tables are one of Excel's most powerful features for data analysis. They allow you to summarize and analyze large datasets quickly and easily, enabling you to identify trends, patterns, and outliers in your data. Pivot charts provide graphical representations of pivot table data, making it easier to visualize and understand complex datasets.

Statistical Analysis:

Excel offers a range of statistical functions for analyzing data, including measures of central tendency, dispersion, correlation, and regression. You can use these functions to calculate summary statistics, perform hypothesis tests, and explore relationships between variables.

What-If Analysis:

Excel's what-if analysis tools allow you to explore different scenarios by changing input values and observing the impact on calculated results. You can use data tables, scenarios, and goal seek to perform sensitivity analysis, scenario analysis, and optimization.

Data Visualization:

Excel provides a variety of chart types and customization options for visualizing data. You can create bar charts, line charts, pie charts, scatter plots, and more, and customize the appearance and layout of your charts to communicate your findings effectively.

By leveraging Excel's data analysis tools and techniques, you can gain valuable insights from your data, make informed decisions, and drive business success. Whether you're a business analyst, financial analyst, or data scientist, Excel provides a versatile platform for exploring, analyzing, and visualizing data in a wide range of contexts.

Pivot Tables and Pivot Charts

Pivot tables and pivot charts are two of Excel's most powerful features for data analysis and visualization. They allow you to summarize and analyze large datasets quickly and easily, enabling you to gain valuable insights and identify trends in your data. Let's explore how pivot tables and pivot charts work and how you can use them to analyze your data effectively:

Pivot Tables:

Pivot tables are interactive tables that allow you to summarize and analyze data from a larger dataset. They provide a flexible and dynamic way to rearrange and summarize data, making it easy to identify patterns, trends, and outliers.

- Creating a Pivot Table: To create a pivot table, simply select the range of data you want to analyze, go to the "Insert" tab, and click "PivotTable." Excel will then prompt you to select the range of data and the location where you want to place the pivot table.

- Customizing a Pivot Table: Once you've created a pivot table, you can customize it by dragging and dropping fields from your dataset into the rows, columns, values, and filters areas of the pivot table layout. You can also apply filters, sort data, and format the pivot table to meet your specific analysis needs.

- Analyzing Data with Pivot Tables: With a pivot table, you can quickly summarize and analyze your data by calculating sums, averages, counts, and other aggregate functions. You can also group data by date, category, or other criteria to gain deeper insights into your dataset.

Pivot Charts:

Pivot charts are graphical representations of pivot table data, making it easier to visualize and understand complex datasets. They allow you to create dynamic charts that update automatically as you change the underlying pivot table.

- Creating a Pivot Chart: To create a pivot chart, simply select a cell within your pivot table, go to the "Insert" tab, and click on the type of chart you want to create. Excel will then generate a chart based on the data in your pivot table.

- Customizing a Pivot Chart: Like pivot tables, you can customize pivot charts by changing the chart type, formatting the axes, adding titles and labels, and applying different chart styles. You can also interact with the pivot chart by filtering data and drilling down into specific details.

- Analyzing Data with Pivot Charts: Pivot charts allow you to visualize trends, patterns, and outliers in your data more effectively than traditional charts. You can use pivot charts to compare different categories, track changes over time, and identify correlations between variables.

By leveraging pivot tables and pivot charts, you can analyze large datasets more efficiently, gain deeper insights into your data, and communicate your findings more effectively to stakeholders. Whether you're a business analyst, financial analyst, or data scientist, pivot tables and pivot charts are essential tools for data analysis and visualization in Excel.

Advanced Charting Techniques

Excel offers a wide array of advanced charting techniques that enable you to create visually compelling and insightful visualizations of your data. These techniques go beyond basic chart types, allowing you to convey complex information effectively and make your data analysis more impactful.

Let's explore some advanced charting techniques in Excel:

Combination Charts:

Combination charts allow you to display multiple data series on a single chart, combining different chart types (e.g., line, bar, and column) within the same chart. This enables you to compare different datasets or variables more easily and identify relationships between them.

Trendlines and Error Bars:

Trendlines are useful for visualizing trends and patterns in your data over time. Excel allows you to add trendlines to your charts, such as linear, exponential, logarithmic, and polynomial trendlines, helping you to identify and understand trends more effectively. Error bars are another useful feature that allow you to display variability or uncertainty in your data, making your charts more informative and insightful.

Sparklines:

Sparklines are small, compact charts that can be embedded directly within cells, providing a quick visual summary of your data. They are particularly useful for displaying trends or patterns in a series of data points, such as stock prices, sales figures, or temperature fluctuations. Sparklines are a great way to add context and visual interest to your Excel spreadsheets without taking up much space.

Waterfall Charts:

Waterfall charts are ideal for visualizing changes in data over time or from one category to another. They are commonly used in financial analysis to illustrate the cumulative effect of positive and negative changes on a starting value. Excel offers built-in templates for creating waterfall charts, making it easy to visualize changes in your data and identify key drivers of change.

Heatmaps and Geographic Maps:

Heatmaps are useful for visualizing large datasets and identifying patterns or trends in your data. They use color gradients to represent data values, with darker colors indicating higher values and lighter colors indicating lower values. Excel also allows you to create geographic maps based on your data, enabling you to visualize spatial patterns or distributions in your data more effectively.

Dynamic Charts and Interactive Dashboards:

Excel offers features such as dynamic charts and interactive dashboards that allow you to create dynamic, interactive visualizations of your data. You can use features like slicers, timelines, and scroll bars to filter and interact with your data dynamically, making your charts more engaging and actionable.

By leveraging these advanced charting techniques in Excel, you can create visually stunning and informative visualizations of your data, enabling you to communicate your findings more effectively and make better-informed decisions. Whether you're analyzing financial data, tracking sales performance, or visualizing trends over time, Excel provides the tools you need to create impactful charts and visualizations that bring your data to life.

Macros and VBA for Automation

Excel's built-in programming language, Visual Basic for Applications (VBA), empowers users to automate repetitive tasks, customize functionality, and extend Excel's capabilities beyond its standard features. By leveraging macros and VBA, you can streamline workflows, increase productivity, and eliminate manual errors.

How macros and VBA can be used for automation in Excel:

Creating Macros:

Macros are sequences of recorded actions that can be replayed to automate tasks in Excel. You can record a macro to perform a series of actions, such as formatting cells, copying and pasting data, or running calculations, and then replay the macro whenever you need to repeat those actions.

Editing Macros in VBA Editor:

The VBA Editor provides a powerful environment for creating, editing, and managing macros. You can open the VBA Editor by pressing Alt + F11 or by going to the "Developer" tab and clicking on "Visual Basic." In the VBA Editor, you can write, edit, and debug VBA code to customize your macros and add advanced functionality.

Writing VBA Code:

VBA (Visual Basic for Applications) is a programming language that allows you to write custom scripts to automate tasks in Excel. With VBA, you can create sophisticated macros that perform complex calculations, manipulate data, interact with other applications, and more. VBA provides a wide range of built-in functions and objects that you can use to manipulate Excel workbooks, worksheets, ranges, charts, and other objects.

Automating Data Processing Tasks:

VBA can be used to automate a wide range of data processing tasks in Excel, such as data cleaning, data validation, data manipulation, and data analysis. For example, you can write VBA code to import data from external sources, clean and format the data, perform calculations and analysis, and generate reports or visualizations automatically.

Customizing User Interfaces:

VBA can also be used to customize Excel's user interface by adding custom buttons, menus, and dialog boxes. You can create user-friendly interfaces that streamline workflows and make it easier for users to interact with Excel spreadsheets. For example, you can create a custom toolbar with buttons that trigger specific macros, or a custom form with input fields for entering data.

Integration with Other Applications:

VBA enables seamless integration between Excel and other applications, allowing you to automate cross-application workflows and exchange data between different systems. For example, you can write VBA code to interact with databases, web services, or external APIs, enabling you to pull in data from external sources or push data to other systems automatically.

By mastering macros and VBA in Excel, you can unlock a world of automation possibilities, streamlining your workflows, increasing productivity, and eliminating manual errors. Whether you're a beginner or an experienced programmer, macros and VBA provide powerful tools for automating tasks and customizing Excel to suit your specific needs.

Using Excel for Financial Modeling

Excel is widely regarded as one of the most powerful tools for financial modeling due to its flexibility, versatility, and robust features. Financial modeling involves creating mathematical representations of financial scenarios to analyze and forecast the performance of businesses, investments, or financial instruments. Excel provides a comprehensive suite of functions, tools, and capabilities that make it an ideal platform for building sophisticated financial models. Here's how you can use Excel for financial modeling:

Building Financial Statements:
Excel allows you to create detailed financial statements, including income statements, balance sheets, and cash flow statements. By inputting historical financial data and assumptions about future performance, you can project the financial position and performance of a business over time.

Performing Financial Analysis:
Excel provides a wide range of financial functions and formulas that facilitate various types of financial analysis. You can calculate key financial metrics such as net present value (NPV), internal rate of return (IRR), return on investment (ROI), and profitability ratios. These analyses help assess the viability and profitability of investments, projects, or business ventures.

Scenario Analysis and Sensitivity Analysis:

Excel enables you to conduct scenario analysis and sensitivity analysis to evaluate the impact of different variables or assumptions on financial outcomes. By changing input values such as revenue growth rates, cost structures, or interest rates, you can assess how changes in these variables affect financial performance and risk.

Valuation Modeling:

Excel is widely used for valuation modeling, which involves estimating the value of assets, companies, or investments. Valuation models can include discounted cash flow (DCF) analysis, comparable company analysis (CCA), and precedent transaction analysis (PTA). Excel's built-in functions and tools facilitate complex valuation calculations and methodologies.

Monte Carlo Simulation:

Excel supports Monte Carlo simulation, a statistical technique used to assess the impact of uncertainty and risk on financial outcomes. By running multiple iterations of a model with randomly generated inputs, you can generate probabilistic forecasts and assess the probability distribution of financial outcomes.

Financial Reporting and Dashboards:
Excel allows you to create dynamic financial reports and dashboards that provide real-time insights into financial performance. You can use features like pivot tables, charts, and conditional formatting to visualize financial data and communicate key metrics and trends effectively.

Version Control and Auditing:
Excel's auditing tools and version control features enable you to track changes to financial models, identify errors or discrepancies, and ensure data integrity. You can use features like cell auditing, formula tracing, and version history to maintain accuracy and transparency in financial modeling processes.

By leveraging Excel for financial modeling, you can analyze complex financial scenarios, make informed decisions, and drive business success. Whether you're a financial analyst, investment banker, or corporate finance professional, Excel provides the tools and capabilities you need to build robust and reliable financial models that support strategic decision-making and planning.

Chapter 4: Practical Applications of Excel

Excel is more than just a spreadsheet program; it's a versatile tool that finds applications in various industries and domains. From simple calculations to complex data analysis and visualization, Excel offers a wide range of features and functionalities that make it indispensable for businesses, educators, researchers, and individuals alike.

Let's explore some practical applications of Excel:

1. Financial Management: Excel is widely used for financial management tasks such as budgeting, forecasting, and financial reporting. Businesses use Excel to create budgets, track expenses, analyze cash flow, and generate financial statements. Excel's built-in financial functions and templates simplify complex calculations and enable accurate financial analysis.

2. Data Analysis and Reporting: Excel is a powerful tool for data analysis and reporting. Researchers, analysts, and professionals across various industries use Excel to analyze datasets, perform statistical analysis, and generate reports. Excel's pivot tables, charts, and conditional formatting features make it easy to visualize data and communicate insights effectively.

3. Project Management: Excel is commonly used for project management tasks such as project planning, scheduling, and tracking. Project managers use Excel to create Gantt charts, project timelines, and task lists to organize and monitor project activities. Excel's collaboration features, such as shared workbooks and online access, facilitate teamwork and communication among project stakeholders.

4. Inventory Management: Excel is often used for inventory management tasks such as inventory tracking, stock control, and order management. Businesses use Excel to record inventory levels, track stock movements, and generate inventory reports. Excel's formulas and functions enable automated calculations and alerts for inventory management tasks.

5. Academic and Educational Purposes: Excel is widely used in education for academic purposes such as data analysis, scientific calculations, and grading. Teachers and students use Excel to perform experiments, analyze research data, and create interactive learning materials. Excel's versatility and ease of use make it a valuable tool for teaching and learning across various subjects and disciplines.

6. Human Resource Management: Excel is employed for human resource management tasks such as employee scheduling, payroll processing, and performance tracking. HR professionals use Excel to manage employee records, calculate salaries and benefits, and generate HR reports. Excel's templates and formulas streamline HR processes and facilitate compliance with regulatory requirements.

7. Marketing and Sales Analysis: Excel is used for marketing and sales analysis tasks such as customer segmentation, campaign tracking, and sales forecasting. Marketing and sales professionals use Excel to analyze customer data, track marketing campaigns, and forecast sales performance. Excel's data visualization tools help identify trends, patterns, and opportunities for marketing and sales optimization.

8. Personal Finance Management: Excel is widely used for personal finance management tasks such as budgeting, expense tracking, and investment analysis. Individuals use Excel to create personal budgets, track spending, and monitor investment portfolios. Excel's templates and financial functions enable individuals to manage their finances effectively and make informed financial decisions.

Excel's practical applications extend across a wide range of industries and domains, making it an indispensable tool for businesses, educators, researchers, and individuals. Whether you're managing finances, analyzing data, or organizing projects, Excel provides the flexibility, functionality, and reliability you need to accomplish your tasks efficiently and effectively.

Business Applications

Excel is a cornerstone tool for businesses of all sizes, providing a versatile platform for a myriad of critical functions across various departments. From financial analysis to project management, Excel's robust features and user-friendly interface make it indispensable for streamlining processes, analyzing data, and making informed decisions.

Let's delve into some key business applications of Excel:

1. Financial Analysis and Reporting:

Excel is extensively used for financial analysis, budgeting, forecasting, and reporting. Finance departments rely on Excel to create income statements, balance sheets, cash flow statements, and other financial reports. Its powerful functions and formulas enable complex calculations, such as net present value (NPV), internal rate of return (IRR), and financial ratios, facilitating comprehensive financial analysis and decision-making.

2. Data Management and Analysis:

Excel serves as a central hub for managing and analyzing business data. It allows users to organize large datasets, perform data cleansing and manipulation, and derive valuable insights through pivot tables, charts, and advanced analysis tools. From tracking sales performance to analyzing market trends, Excel empowers businesses to extract actionable intelligence from their data.

3. Project Planning and Tracking:

Excel is a go-to tool for project managers to plan, organize, and track project activities. Gantt charts, project timelines, and task lists can be easily created to visualize project schedules, monitor progress, and allocate resources efficiently. Excel's collaborative features enable real-time updates and communication among team members, fostering transparency and accountability in project management.

4. Inventory Management and Supply Chain Optimization:

Excel facilitates inventory management tasks such as tracking stock levels, managing purchase orders, and optimizing supply chain operations. Businesses use Excel to monitor inventory turnover, forecast demand, and ensure optimal stock levels to meet customer demand while minimizing carrying costs. Excel's formulas and templates streamline inventory management processes and support data-driven decision-making in supply chain management.

5. Sales and Customer Relationship Management:

Excel plays a crucial role in sales and customer relationship management (CRM) activities. Sales teams utilize Excel to track leads, manage customer information, and analyze sales performance metrics. Excel's sorting, filtering, and data validation features enable efficient lead management and segmentation, while pivot tables and charts facilitate in-depth analysis of sales data and trends.

6. Human Resource Management and Employee Tracking:

Excel aids HR departments in managing employee data, tracking attendance, and evaluating performance. HR professionals use Excel to maintain employee records, calculate payroll, and generate HR reports. Excel's conditional formatting and formulas enable automated workflows for tracking leave balances, managing employee schedules, and conducting performance evaluations.

7. Business Planning and Strategy Development:

Excel serves as a versatile tool for business planning, strategy development, and decision support. Businesses use Excel to create business plans, perform scenario analysis, and evaluate strategic alternatives. Excel's modeling capabilities allow businesses to simulate different scenarios, assess risks, and devise strategies to achieve their goals effectively.

8. Marketing Campaign Analysis and Optimization:

Excel supports marketing teams in analyzing campaign performance, tracking marketing expenses, and optimizing marketing strategies. Marketers use Excel to calculate key performance indicators (KPIs), analyze customer data, and measure ROI on marketing initiatives. Excel's charting tools and data visualization capabilities facilitate the presentation of marketing insights and enable data-driven decision-making in marketing campaigns.

Excel's versatility and functionality make it an indispensable tool for businesses across various industries and departments. Whether it's financial analysis, project management, inventory tracking, or strategic planning, Excel empowers businesses to streamline operations, analyze data effectively, and drive informed decision-making for sustainable growth and success.

Excel for Project Management

Excel for Project Management

Excel is a versatile tool that offers numerous features and functionalities ideal for project management. From planning and scheduling to tracking progress and analyzing data, Excel provides a flexible and customizable platform for managing projects of any size or complexity.

How Excel can be effectively used for project management:

1. Project Planning and Scheduling:
Excel allows you to create detailed project plans and schedules using Gantt charts, timelines, and task lists. You can break down the project into individual tasks, assign responsibilities, set deadlines, and establish dependencies between tasks. Excel's built-in templates and conditional formatting features make it easy to visualize project timelines and identify critical path activities.

2. Task Tracking and Management:

Excel enables you to track the progress of project tasks, monitor deadlines, and manage resource allocation efficiently. You can use spreadsheets to record task statuses, update completion percentages, and track actual vs. planned progress. Conditional formatting and data validation rules can be applied to highlight overdue tasks, identify bottlenecks, and ensure timely completion of project milestones.

3. Resource Allocation and Management:

Excel allows you to manage project resources effectively by tracking resource availability, allocation, and utilization. You can create resource allocation charts, team schedules, and workload matrices to ensure that resources are allocated optimally and that team members are utilized efficiently. Excel's formulas and functions enable you to calculate resource capacities, balance workloads, and identify resource constraints.

4. Budgeting and Cost Tracking:

Excel serves as a valuable tool for budgeting, cost estimation, and tracking project expenses. You can create budget templates, expense trackers, and cost breakdowns to monitor project costs and expenditures. Excel's financial functions and formulas enable you to calculate project budgets, forecast costs, and analyze variances between planned vs. actual expenses, ensuring that projects stay within budget constraints.

5. Risk Management and Issue Tracking:

Excel facilitates risk management and issue tracking by providing a platform to identify, assess, and mitigate project risks and issues. You can create risk registers, issue logs, and mitigation plans to document and monitor risks throughout the project lifecycle. Excel's sorting, filtering, and charting capabilities enable you to prioritize risks, track mitigation efforts, and communicate risk status effectively to stakeholders.

6. Communication and Collaboration:

Excel supports communication and collaboration among project stakeholders by providing features such as shared workbooks, comments, and version history. Team members can collaborate on project documents, update task lists, and share progress updates in real-time using Excel's online collaboration tools. This fosters transparency, accountability, and alignment among project teams, leading to better coordination and decision-making.

7. Reporting and Analysis:

Excel enables you to generate project reports, analyze project performance, and derive insights from project data. You can create dashboards, charts, and pivot tables to visualize project metrics, track key performance indicators (KPIs), and identify trends and patterns in project data. Excel's data analysis tools empower you to conduct root cause analysis, evaluate project risks, and make data-driven decisions to improve project outcomes.

Excel provides a comprehensive platform for project management, offering a wide range of features and functionalities to plan, track, and analyze projects effectively. Whether you're managing tasks, allocating resources, tracking costs, or analyzing risks, Excel's flexibility and versatility make it an indispensable tool for project managers seeking to drive successful project outcomes.

Excel in Data Science and Analysis

While Excel may not be the first tool that comes to mind for data science and analysis, it remains a widely used platform due to its accessibility, versatility, and familiarity to many users. Excel offers a range of features and functionalities that make it suitable for various data analysis tasks, especially for users who are new to data science or working with smaller datasets.

How Excel can be utilized in data science and analysis:

1. Data Import and Cleaning:
Excel allows users to import data from various sources, including databases, text files, and web

pages. Once imported, Excel's data manipulation features enable users to clean and preprocess data, remove duplicates, handle missing values, and format data for analysis.

2. Data Exploration and Visualization:

Excel provides tools for exploring and visualizing data, including pivot tables, charts, and conditional formatting. Users can quickly summarize and visualize data using pivot tables, create various chart types to visualize trends and patterns, and apply conditional formatting to highlight important insights.

3. Statistical Analysis:

Excel offers a range of statistical functions and tools for performing basic statistical analysis, such as calculating descriptive statistics, correlation coefficients, and hypothesis testing. Users can use Excel's statistical functions to analyze data distributions, compare group means, and test hypotheses about population parameters.

4. Regression Analysis:

Excel's regression analysis tools enable users to perform linear and nonlinear regression analysis to model relationships between variables and make predictions. Users can use Excel's regression analysis tool to fit regression models, assess model fit, and interpret regression coefficients to understand the relationship between predictor and outcome variables.

5. Time Series Analysis:

Excel supports time series analysis, allowing users to analyze and forecast time series data using functions such as moving averages, exponential smoothing, and time series regression. Users can use Excel's time series analysis tools to identify trends, seasonality, and anomalies in time series data and make forecasts based on historical patterns.

6. Data Mining and Machine Learning:

While Excel may not offer advanced machine learning capabilities out-of-the-box, users can still perform basic data mining and machine learning tasks using Excel's built-in features and add-ins.

Excel supports tasks such as clustering analysis, classification, and decision tree modeling using add-ins like the Data Analysis ToolPak and third-party plugins.

7. Reporting and Presentation:

Excel's reporting and presentation features enable users to create professional-looking reports and presentations to communicate their findings effectively. Users can customize report layouts, add charts and graphs to visualize data, and use Excel's formatting and styling options to create visually appealing presentations.

8. Integration with Other Tools:

Excel can be integrated with other data science tools and platforms to extend its capabilities. Users can import and export data between Excel and other tools such as Python, R, and SQL to leverage advanced analytics and modeling techniques not natively supported in Excel.

While Excel may not offer the same level of sophistication and scalability as dedicated data science tools and platforms, it remains a valuable tool for data analysis, especially for users who are new to data science or working with smaller datasets. Excel's accessibility, versatility, and familiarity make it an attractive option for performing a wide range of data analysis tasks in various domains and industries.

Personal Finance with Excel

Excel is an invaluable tool for managing personal finances, offering a range of features and functionalities that enable users to track expenses, create budgets, analyze spending patterns, and plan for financial goals effectively. Whether you're budgeting for everyday expenses, tracking investments, or planning for retirement, Excel provides the flexibility and customization options to suit your personal finance needs.

How Excel can be used for personal finance:

1. Budgeting and Expense Tracking:

Excel allows users to create personalized budgets and track expenses across various categories, such as groceries, utilities, transportation, and entertainment. Users can input their income and expenses into Excel spreadsheets, categorize transactions, and monitor spending against budgeted amounts. Excel's formulas and functions enable users to perform calculations, such as summing expenses by category or calculating savings rates.

2. Cash Flow Management:

Excel facilitates cash flow management by helping users track income sources, monitor cash inflows and outflows, and maintain liquidity. Users can create cash flow statements to visualize their monthly income and expenses, identify cash flow trends, and plan for irregular expenses or income fluctuations. Excel's charts and graphs allow users to visualize cash flow patterns and make informed decisions about saving and spending.

3. Debt Management and Loan Amortization:

Excel supports debt management by allowing users to track loans, credit card balances, and other debts. Users can create loan amortization schedules to understand their debt repayment timeline, calculate monthly payments, and track principal and interest payments over time. Excel's financial functions enable users to analyze debt repayment strategies, such as accelerating payments or consolidating debts.

4. Investment Tracking and Portfolio Management:

Excel enables users to track investment portfolios, monitor asset allocation, and analyze investment performance. Users can input investment transactions, such as purchases, sales, and dividends, into Excel spreadsheets and calculate portfolio returns, volatility, and risk-adjusted performance metrics. Excel's charts and graphs allow users to visualize portfolio performance and assess investment strategies.

5. Retirement Planning and Savings Goals:

Excel supports retirement planning by helping users estimate retirement needs, set savings goals, and track progress towards retirement goals. Users can create retirement savings calculators to estimate future retirement expenses, calculate retirement savings required, and determine savings targets based on retirement age and desired lifestyle. Excel's goal-seeking tools enable users to adjust savings contributions to meet retirement goals.

6. Tax Planning and Forecasting:

Excel facilitates tax planning by allowing users to estimate tax liabilities, plan for tax deductions and credits, and forecast tax refunds or payments. Users can create tax planning worksheets to track income sources, deductions, and credits, and estimate tax liabilities based on current tax rates and regulations. Excel's what-if analysis tools enable users to explore different tax scenarios and optimize tax strategies.

7. Financial Goal Setting and Monitoring:

Excel helps users set and monitor financial goals, such as saving for a home, paying off debt, or building an emergency fund. Users can create goal-tracking spreadsheets to set SMART (specific, measurable, achievable, relevant, and time-bound) financial goals, track progress towards goals, and celebrate milestones. Excel's conditional formatting features allow users to visualize goal progress and stay motivated.

Excel provides a powerful platform for managing personal finances, offering tools and capabilities to budget, track expenses, manage debt, analyze investments, plan for retirement, and achieve financial goals. Whether you're a novice or experienced user, Excel's flexibility, customization options, and ease of use make it an indispensable tool for taking control of your personal finances and achieving financial success.

Collaborative Features and Sharing Workbooks

Excel offers a range of collaborative features that enable multiple users to work on the same workbook simultaneously, facilitating teamwork, communication, and productivity. Whether you're collaborating with colleagues on a project, sharing financial data with stakeholders, or working on a budget with family members, Excel's collaborative features make it easy to share workbooks, track changes, and coordinate efforts effectively.

Let's explore some key collaborative features and how to share workbooks in Excel:

1. Real-Time Co-Authoring:

Excel allows multiple users to co-author a workbook in real-time, enabling them to view and edit the same workbook simultaneously. Users can see each other's changes in real-time, track changes made by others, and collaborate seamlessly without worrying about version control or conflicting edits.

2. Share Workbook:

Excel's "Shared Workbook" feature allows users to share workbooks with others, granting them access to view and edit the workbook simultaneously. Users can share workbooks via email, OneDrive, SharePoint, or other cloud storage platforms, making it easy to collaborate with colleagues, clients, or partners regardless of their location.

3. Permissions and Access Control:

Excel allows users to set permissions and access control settings when sharing workbooks, ensuring that only authorized users can view or edit specific parts of the workbook. Users can assign different permission levels, such as "read-only" or "edit," to control who can make changes to the workbook and who can only view the content.

4. Comments and Annotations:

Excel enables users to add comments and annotations to cells, allowing them to provide feedback, ask questions, or clarify information within the workbook. Comments can be used to communicate with collaborators, provide context for specific data points, or track discussions related to the workbook.

5. Track Changes:

Excel's "Track Changes" feature allows users to track changes made to the workbook by different users, including edits, insertions, deletions, and formatting changes. Users can review and accept or reject changes, compare versions of the workbook, and maintain an audit trail of edits made by collaborators.

6. Shared Views and Filters:

Excel allows users to create shared views and filters within a workbook, enabling them to customize the view of the data without affecting other users' views. Shared views and filters can be saved and applied to the workbook, making it easier to focus on specific data subsets or perspectives when collaborating with others.

7. Merge Workbooks:

Excel's "Merge Workbooks" feature allows users to merge changes from multiple copies of the same workbook into a single, master copy. This feature is useful when users have worked on separate copies of the workbook offline and need to consolidate their changes into a single version.

Excel's collaborative features and sharing capabilities empower users to work together seamlessly, regardless of their location or time zone. Whether you're collaborating on a project, sharing financial data, or working on a budget with family members, Excel's collaborative features make it easy to share workbooks, track changes, and coordinate efforts effectively.

Chapter 5: Strategies for Excel Efficiency

Excel is a powerful tool with countless features and capabilities, but maximizing efficiency in Excel requires more than just knowing the basics. By employing the right strategies and techniques, you can streamline your workflow, increase productivity, and accomplish tasks more effectively in Excel.

Here are some strategies to enhance your efficiency in Excel:

1. Keyboard Shortcuts:

Learn and utilize keyboard shortcuts to perform common tasks quickly without relying on the mouse. Keyboard shortcuts such as Ctrl+C for copy, Ctrl+V for paste, and Ctrl+S for save can significantly speed up your workflow.

2. Named Ranges:

Use named ranges to assign descriptive names to cells or ranges of cells. Named ranges make formulas more readable and easier to understand,

and they can also save time by eliminating the need to reference cell addresses directly.

3. Excel Tables:

Convert your data into Excel tables to take advantage of built-in features such as automatic filtering, sorting, and totaling. Excel tables make it easier to manage and analyze large datasets, and they automatically expand or contract as you add or remove data.

4. Conditional Formatting:

Apply conditional formatting to highlight important information in your data, such as outliers, trends, or specific values. Conditional formatting helps draw attention to key insights and makes your data more visually appealing and easier to interpret.

5. Pivot Tables and Pivot Charts:

Master the use of pivot tables and pivot charts to analyze and visualize data quickly and dynamically. Pivot tables allow you to summarize and aggregate large datasets, while pivot charts provide visual representations of your data, making it easier to identify trends and patterns.

6. Formula Auditing Tools:

Use Excel's formula auditing tools to trace precedents and dependents, identify errors in formulas, and troubleshoot complex calculations. Tools such as Trace Precedents and Trace Dependents help you understand how data flows through your workbook and identify potential sources of errors.

7. Data Validation:

Implement data validation rules to control the type and format of data entered into your spreadsheets. Data validation helps prevent errors and ensures data consistency by restricting input to predefined criteria, such as dates, numbers, or list values.

8. Excel Add-Ins:

Explore and leverage Excel add-ins to extend Excel's capabilities and automate repetitive tasks. Add-ins such as Power Query, Power Pivot, and Solver provide advanced data analysis and modeling features that can save time and improve efficiency.

9. Custom Templates and Macros:

Create custom templates and macros for recurring tasks or workflows to automate repetitive processes and save time. Templates allow you to standardize formatting and layout, while macros enable you to record and replay sequences of actions to automate complex tasks.

10. Regular Training and Practice:

Continuously improve your Excel skills through regular training and practice. Explore new features, experiment with advanced techniques, and stay updated on the latest tips and tricks to become more proficient and efficient in Excel.

By implementing these strategies and techniques, you can enhance your efficiency in Excel and accomplish tasks more effectively, whether you're analyzing data, creating reports, or managing projects. With practice and perseverance, you can become a more proficient Excel user and unlock its full potential for productivity and success.

Time-Saving Tips and Tricks

Excel is a versatile tool that offers numerous features and functionalities to streamline your workflow and save time on various tasks. Whether you're crunching numbers, analyzing data, or creating reports, these time-saving tips and tricks will help you work more efficiently in Excel:

1. Autofill and Flash Fill:

Utilize Autofill to quickly fill cells with sequences, such as numbers, dates, or custom lists, by dragging the fill handle. Alternatively, use Flash Fill to automatically recognize patterns and fill adjacent cells with corresponding data.

2. Quick Analysis Tool:

Take advantage of the Quick Analysis tool (Ctrl + Q) to access a variety of formatting, charting, and data analysis options, saving time on common tasks like creating charts, applying conditional formatting, and summarizing data.

3. Keyboard Shortcuts:

Learn and use keyboard shortcuts to perform tasks more efficiently. For example, Ctrl + C for copy, Ctrl + V for paste, Ctrl + Z for undo, and Ctrl + Y for redo are commonly used shortcuts that can significantly speed up your workflow.

4. Excel Templates:

Start with pre-built Excel templates for common tasks such as budgets, calendars, invoices, and project plans. Templates provide a starting point and can save you time by eliminating the need to create documents from scratch.

5. Custom Number Formatting:

Use custom number formatting to display data in a more readable and visually appealing format. For example, you can format dates, currencies, percentages, and fractions according to your preferences without altering the underlying data.

6. Name Manager:

Manage named ranges more efficiently using the Name Manager (Formulas > Name Manager). The Name Manager allows you to view, edit, and organize named ranges, making it easier to work with complex formulas and references.

7. Filter and Sort:

Quickly filter and sort data using Excel's built-in filtering and sorting features. Use the Filter button in the Data tab to apply filters to your data and narrow down results based on specific criteria.

8. Conditional Formatting Rules:

Apply conditional formatting rules to highlight important trends, outliers, or exceptions in your data automatically. You can use preset rules or create custom rules based on specific conditions to visually identify key insights.

9. Excel Tables:

Convert your data into Excel tables (Ctrl + T) to take advantage of built-in features such as filtering, sorting, and totaling. Excel tables automatically expand or contract as you add or remove data, making it easier to manage and analyze large datasets.

10. Use Excel Add-Ins:

Explore Excel add-ins such as Power Query, Power Pivot, and Solver to extend Excel's capabilities and automate repetitive tasks. Add-ins provide advanced data analysis and modeling features that can save time and improve efficiency.

By incorporating these time-saving tips and tricks into your Excel workflow, you can work more efficiently and effectively, allowing you to accomplish tasks faster and focus on more important aspects of your work. Whether you're a beginner or an experienced Excel user, these strategies will help you maximize productivity and get the most out of Excel's powerful features.

Keyboard Shortcuts and Quick Access Toolbar

Keyboard shortcuts and the Quick Access Toolbar (QAT) are essential tools in Excel for improving productivity and efficiency. They allow you to perform common tasks quickly without the need to navigate through menus or use the mouse extensively.

How you can leverage keyboard shortcuts and the Quick Access Toolbar to streamline your workflow in Excel:

Keyboard Shortcuts:

1. Copy, Cut, Paste: Ctrl + C, Ctrl + X, Ctrl + V

2. Undo, Redo: Ctrl + Z, Ctrl + Y

3. Select Entire Column, Row: Ctrl + Spacebar, Shift + Spacebar

4. Insert New Worksheet: Shift + F11

5. Fill Down, Fill Right: Ctrl + D, Ctrl + R

6. Autofill: Ctrl + E

7. Go to Next Sheet, Previous Sheet: Ctrl + Page Down, Ctrl + Page Up

8. Select All Cells with Data: Ctrl + Shift + Arrow Key (Up, Down, Left, Right)

9. Format Painter: Ctrl + Shift + C (Copy Format), Ctrl + Shift + V (Paste Format)

10. Open Format Cells Dialog Box: Ctrl + 1

Quick Access Toolbar (QAT):

1. Customize QAT: Right-click any command on the Ribbon and select "Add to Quick Access Toolbar" to add it to the QAT.

2. Keyboard Shortcuts for QAT: After adding a command to the QAT, press Alt + the corresponding number (1-9) to activate it.

3. Positioning QAT: Customize the position of the QAT by clicking the drop-down arrow at the end of the toolbar and selecting "Show Below the Ribbon" or "Show Above the Ribbon."

4. Save Time with QAT: Add frequently used commands to the QAT to access them with a single click, eliminating the need to navigate through Ribbon tabs.

5. Sync QAT Settings: Customize the QAT on one computer and sync the settings to other computers using Excel's options for customizing the Ribbon and QAT.

By mastering keyboard shortcuts and customizing the Quick Access Toolbar to suit your workflow, you can significantly improve your productivity and efficiency in Excel. These tools allow you to perform tasks more quickly and efficiently, ultimately saving you time and enhancing your overall experience with Excel.

Best Practices for Data Entry and Management

Effective data entry and management are essential for maintaining accurate and organized data in Excel. By following best practices, you can ensure data integrity, consistency, and usability, making it easier to analyze and work with your data.

The best practices for data entry and management in Excel:

1. Plan Your Data Structure:

Before entering data into Excel, carefully plan the structure of your workbook, including the layout of worksheets, tables, and named ranges. Determine how you will organize your data to facilitate analysis and reporting.

2. Use Consistent Data Formats:

Maintain consistency in data formats to ensure uniformity and readability. Use consistent date formats, number formats, and text conventions throughout your workbook to prevent errors and confusion.

3. Validate Data Input:

Implement data validation rules to control the type and format of data entered into cells. Use data validation to restrict input to specific values, ranges, or lists, reducing the likelihood of errors and inconsistencies.

4. Avoid Merged Cells:

Avoid merging cells in Excel, as it can complicate data entry, sorting, and filtering. Merged cells can also cause formatting issues and make it challenging to work with data effectively.

5. Organize Data with Tables:

Convert your data into Excel tables (Ctrl + T) to take advantage of built-in features such as filtering, sorting, and totaling. Tables automatically expand or contract as you add or remove data, making it easier to manage and analyze large datasets.

6. Use Descriptive Headers:

Use descriptive headers for columns and rows to provide context and clarity to your data. Choose meaningful column headers that accurately describe the data they contain, making it easier to understand and analyze.

7. Avoid Hardcoding Values:

Avoid hardcoding values directly into formulas or cells. Instead, use named ranges or cell references to refer to data stored elsewhere in your workbook.

This allows for easier updates and reduces the risk of errors.

8. Document Data Sources and Assumptions:

Document the sources of your data and any assumptions made during data entry or analysis. Include comments or annotations to provide context and explain calculations or interpretations.

9. Regularly Review and Clean Data:

Regularly review and clean your data to remove duplicates, correct errors, and update outdated information. Use Excel's data cleaning tools, such as Remove Duplicates and Text to Columns, to clean and standardize your data.

10. Backup Your Workbook:

Regularly backup your Excel workbook to prevent data loss due to unexpected errors or accidents. Save multiple versions of your workbook or use cloud storage services to ensure your data is protected and accessible.

By following these best practices, you can maintain accurate, organized, and reliable data in Excel, making it easier to analyze, report, and derive insights from your data. Consistent data entry and management practices are essential for ensuring data integrity and maximizing the effectiveness of your Excel workbooks.

Troubleshooting Common Issues

Even with its versatility, Excel users may encounter common issues that impede their workflow. Knowing how to troubleshoot these issues can save time and frustration.

Here are solutions to some common Excel problems:

1. Slow Performance:
   - **Solution:** Close unnecessary applications and files to free up system resources. Consider optimizing your workbook by removing excess

formatting, reducing the number of formulas, and limiting volatile functions.

2. Formulas Not Calculating:

- **Solution:** Check if calculation mode is set to manual. Press F9 to manually recalculate formulas or go to Formulas > Calculation Options and select "Automatic." Ensure that cells referenced in formulas contain valid data and are not formatted as text.

3. Excel Freezes or Crashes:

- **Solution:** Save your work frequently to avoid losing data. Close other applications running in the background to free up memory. Update Excel and your operating system to the latest version to resolve compatibility issues.

4. VALUE! or REF! Errors:

- **Solution:** These errors occur when Excel cannot recognize values or references in formulas. Check if cells referenced in formulas contain valid data or are not missing. Use functions like IFERROR or ISERROR to handle errors gracefully.

5. Pivot Table Errors:

- **Solution:** Refresh your pivot table to update it with the latest data. Ensure that the source data range is correct and does not include blank rows or columns. Check for any filters applied to the pivot table that may affect the results.

6. Printing Issues:

- **Solution:** Preview your worksheet before printing to ensure proper formatting. Adjust print settings such as page orientation, margins, and scaling as needed. Check if the printer driver is up-to-date and compatible with Excel.

7. Data Loss:

- **Solution:** Enable AutoRecover to automatically save a backup of your workbook at regular intervals. Use cloud storage services like OneDrive or Google Drive to store and sync your Excel files securely. Consider implementing version control to track changes and restore previous versions if needed.

8. Corrupted Workbook:

- **Solution:** Attempt to open the corrupted workbook in Excel's Safe Mode by holding down the Ctrl key while launching Excel. Use the Open and Repair feature to repair the workbook. If unsuccessful, try to recover data from a backup or use third-party recovery tools.

9. Incorrect Sorting or Filtering:

- **Solution:** Check if the sorting or filtering criteria are correctly applied. Ensure that there are no hidden rows or columns that may affect sorting or filtering results. Reset sorting or filtering by selecting the "Clear" option in the Sort or Filter dropdown menus.

10. Inconsistent Formatting:

- **Solution:** Use Excel's Format Painter tool to copy formatting from one cell to another. Clear formatting from cells by selecting Clear Formats in the Editing group on the Home tab. Apply cell styles or conditional formatting to maintain consistency across your workbook.

Applying these troubleshooting techniques, you can overcome common Excel issues and ensure a smoother experience while working with your data. If you encounter more complex issues, consider consulting Excel's help documentation or reaching out to online forums and communities for further assistance.

Enhancing Productivity with Add-ins and Plugins

Add-ins and plugins offer additional features and functionalities that can enhance productivity and extend the capabilities of Excel beyond its built-in tools. By leveraging these external tools, users can streamline workflows, automate tasks, and unlock new possibilities for data analysis and visualization.

Some ways to enhance productivity with add-ins and plugins in Excel:

1. Power Query:

Power Query is a powerful data transformation tool that allows users to import, clean, and shape data from various sources. With Power Query, you can easily combine data from multiple files or databases, perform complex transformations, and create reusable queries to automate data preparation tasks.

2. Power Pivot:

Power Pivot is an advanced data modeling tool that enables users to create sophisticated data models and perform powerful analysis using large datasets. With Power Pivot, you can create relationships between tables, write custom calculations using DAX (Data Analysis Expressions), and build interactive reports and dashboards.

3. Solver:

Solver is an optimization tool that allows users to find the optimal solution to complex problems by adjusting input variables based on specified constraints and objectives. With Solver, you can perform linear programming, nonlinear optimization, and what-if analysis to optimize decisions and resource allocation.

4. Analysis ToolPak:

The Analysis ToolPak is a collection of statistical, financial, and engineering functions that extends Excel's built-in functions. With the Analysis ToolPak, you can perform advanced data analysis tasks such as regression analysis, hypothesis testing, and time series forecasting without writing complex formulas.

5. Excel Add-ins from Third-party Providers:

Explore a wide range of Excel add-ins available from third-party providers to enhance specific functionalities or address niche requirements. These add-ins offer features such as data visualization, charting, reporting, and automation, catering to diverse needs and industries.

6. Charting Tools:

Excel add-ins such as Tableau, Power BI, and Zoho Analytics offer advanced charting and visualization capabilities that go beyond Excel's native charting tools. These tools allow users to create interactive dashboards, drill-down reports, and dynamic visualizations to gain deeper insights from their data.

7. Data Connectivity Plugins:

Plugins like ODBC (Open Database Connectivity) drivers and connectors enable Excel to connect to external data sources such as databases, cloud storage services, and web APIs. These plugins facilitate seamless data integration and enable real-time access to external data for analysis and reporting.

8. Automation Plugins:

Plugins like Zapier, Microsoft Flow (now called Power Automate), and Automate.io enable users to automate repetitive tasks and streamline workflows by connecting Excel with other applications and services. These plugins allow users to create automated workflows, trigger actions based on predefined conditions, and eliminate manual data entry and processing tasks.

9. Collaboration and Sharing Plugins:

Plugins like Google Workspace (formerly G Suite) integration, Dropbox integration, and SharePoint integration enable users to collaborate on Excel workbooks in real-time, share files securely, and access documents from any device or platform. These plugins facilitate seamless collaboration and communication among team members, regardless of their location or device.

10. Training and Support Resources:

Take advantage of training courses, tutorials, and support resources provided by add-in developers to learn how to use these tools effectively. Many add-in developers offer comprehensive documentation, video tutorials, and online forums where users can get help and support from experts and fellow users.

By leveraging add-ins and plugins in Excel, users can enhance productivity, streamline workflows, and unlock new possibilities for data analysis, visualization, and automation. Whether you're a beginner or an advanced user, exploring and integrating these external tools into your Excel workflow can help you work more efficiently and effectively with your data.

Appendix

In this appendix, you'll find additional resources and references to further enhance your Excel skills, troubleshoot issues, and explore advanced topics. Whether you're looking for training materials, documentation, or online communities, these resources can provide valuable support and guidance for your Excel journey.

1. Excel Help Documentation:

Access Excel's built-in help documentation for comprehensive information on features, functions, and troubleshooting tips. Use the Help menu or press F1 to search for topics and find answers to your questions directly within Excel.

2. Microsoft Office Support Website:

Visit the Microsoft Office Support website for official documentation, tutorials, and troubleshooting guides for Excel and other Office applications. Explore articles, how-to guides, and community forums to find solutions to common issues and learn best practices.

3. Online Training Courses:

Enroll in online training courses offered by platforms such as LinkedIn Learning, Udemy, and Coursera to deepen your Excel knowledge and skills. Courses range from beginner to advanced levels and cover topics such as data analysis, pivot tables, VBA programming, and more.

4. Excel User Forums and Communities:

Join Excel user forums and communities such as MrExcel, Excel Forum, and Reddit's r/excel to connect with fellow users, ask questions, and share knowledge. Participating in discussions and forums can provide valuable insights, tips, and solutions from experienced users.

5. Excel Blogs and Websites:

Follow Excel blogs and websites such as ExcelJet, Chandoo, and Excel Campus for tutorials, tips, and tricks on using Excel effectively. These resources regularly publish articles, tutorials, and videos covering a wide range of Excel topics and techniques.

6. Excel Add-in Documentation:

Refer to documentation and user guides provided by add-in developers for detailed information on installing, configuring, and using Excel add-ins. Many add-in developers offer comprehensive documentation, tutorials, and support resources to help users get started and troubleshoot issues.

7. YouTube Channels and Video Tutorials:

Explore YouTube channels such as ExcelIsFun, MyOnlineTrainingHub, and Leila Gharani for video tutorials and demonstrations on Excel tips, tricks, and techniques. Video tutorials provide step-by-step guidance on using Excel features and functions effectively.

8. Excel Books and Publications:

Invest in Excel books and publications authored by experts in the field for in-depth coverage of Excel concepts, techniques, and best practices. Whether you're looking for beginner guides, advanced reference books, or specialized topics, there are numerous books available to suit your needs.

9. Microsoft Office Blog:

Follow the Microsoft Office Blog for updates, announcements, and tips on using Excel and other Office applications. The blog covers product updates, feature releases, customer stories, and best practices for maximizing productivity with Excel.

10. Online Excel Tools and Calculators:

Explore online Excel tools and calculators for specific tasks such as financial calculations, statistical analysis, and data visualization. Websites like Excel Online, Exceljet, and Excel Easy offer a range of free tools and resources to help users perform common Excel tasks and calculations.

The appendix provides a curated list of additional resources and references to support your Excel journey, whether you're a beginner looking to learn the basics or an advanced user seeking to expand your skills. By exploring these resources, you can enhance your Excel proficiency, troubleshoot issues, and stay up-to-date with the latest developments in Excel.

Excel Formula Cheat Sheet

Excel formulas are powerful tools for performing calculations, manipulating data, and analyzing information. This cheat sheet provides a quick reference guide to some of the most commonly used Excel formulas and functions:

1. SUM:
Calculates the sum of a range of cells.
```excel
=SUM(A1:A10)
```

2. AVERAGE:
Calculates the average of a range of cells.
```excel
=AVERAGE(B1:B10)
```

3. MAX:

Returns the largest value in a range of cells.

```excel
=MAX(C1:C10)
```

4. MIN:

Returns the smallest value in a range of cells.

```excel
=MIN(D1:D10)
```

5. IF:

Performs a logical test and returns one value if the test is true and another if false.

```excel
=IF(E1>10, "Yes", "No")
```

6. VLOOKUP:

Searches for a value in the first column of a table and returns a value in the same row from another column.

```excel
```

```
=VLOOKUP(F1, A1:B10, 2, FALSE)
```
```

### 7. CONCATENATE:

Join two or more text strings into one string.
```excel
=CONCATENATE("Hello ", "World")
```

8. COUNT:

Counts the number of cells in a range that contain numbers.
```excel
=COUNT(G1:G10)
```

9. DATE:

Returns the serial number of a particular date.
```excel
=DATE(2022, 5, 30)
```

10. TODAY:

Returns the current date.
```

```excel
=TODAY()
```

11. NOW:

Returns the current date and time.

```excel
=NOW()
```

12. LEFT:

Returns the leftmost characters from a text string.

```excel
=LEFT(H1, 5)
```

13. RIGHT:

Returns the rightmost characters from a text string.

```excel
=RIGHT(I1, 3)
```

14. LEN:

Returns the number of characters in a text string.

```excel
=LEN(J1)
```

15. INDEX/MATCH:

Uses the MATCH function to find the position of a value in a range, then uses the INDEX function to return the value at that position.

```excel
=INDEX(A1:A10, MATCH(K1, B1:B10, 0))
```

16. INDIRECT:

Returns the reference specified by a text string.

```excel
=INDIRECT("L1")
```

17. RANK:

Returns the rank of a number in a list of numbers.

```excel
```

=RANK(M1, N1:N10)
```

## 18. CHOOSE:

Returns a value from a list of values based on a given position.

```excel
=CHOOSE(O1, P1, Q1, R1)
```

19. ROUND:

Rounds a number to a specified number of digits.

```excel
=ROUND(SQRT(25), 0)
```

20. IFERROR:

Returns a value you specify if a formula evaluates to an error; otherwise, it returns the result of the formula.

```excel
=IFERROR(1/0, "Error")
```
```

Note: Replace cell references (e.g., A1, B1) and values with your actual data when using these formulas.

Common Error Messages and Solutions

Encountering error messages in Excel is common, but understanding their causes and solutions can help you troubleshoot and resolve issues efficiently.

Some of the most common Excel error messages and their solutions:

1. DIV/0!:

Cause: Occurs when attempting to divide a number by zero.

Solution: Check the divisor (denominator) in your formula and ensure it is not zero. Use the IFERROR function to handle division by zero gracefully.

2. VALUE!:

Cause: Indicates that Excel cannot interpret the values in a formula.

Solution: Check for invalid data types or incorrect arguments in your formula. Ensure that cell references contain valid data.

3. REF!:

Cause: Occurs when a cell reference is invalid or refers to a deleted cell or range.

Solution: Review the cell references in your formulas and correct any errors. Check for deleted rows or columns that may be causing the reference error.

4. NAME?:

Cause: Occurs when Excel does not recognize a text string as a valid function or named range.

Solution: Check for spelling errors in function names or named ranges. Ensure that function names are spelled correctly and that named ranges exist in your workbook.

5. N/A:

Cause: Indicates that Excel cannot find a value, such as when using the VLOOKUP or MATCH functions.

Solution: Check the lookup value or search criteria in your formula and verify that it exists in the data range. Ensure that the lookup column is sorted correctly for functions like VLOOKUP.

6. NUM!:

Cause: Occurs when a numeric value is invalid or results in an error, such as exceeding Excel's numeric limits.

Solution: Check for mathematical errors in your formulas, such as exceeding the maximum number of digits or performing calculations with incompatible data types.

7. NULL!:

Cause: Indicates an invalid intersection of two ranges in a formula.

Solution: Review the range references in your formula and ensure that they intersect properly. Verify that there are no missing or overlapping ranges causing the error.

8. SPILL!:

Cause: Occurs when a spill range overflows due to excessive data or incorrect formula inputs.

Solution: Review the spill range and adjust the formula inputs or criteria to prevent overflow. Ensure that the formula is correctly structured to handle the expected data.

9. Circular Reference Warning:

Cause: Indicates that a formula refers to its own cell or creates a circular reference loop.

Solution: Review the formulas in your worksheet and eliminate circular references by restructuring the formulas or removing unnecessary dependencies.

10. File Corruption Warning:

Cause: Occurs when Excel detects corruption in a workbook, preventing it from opening properly.

Solution: Attempt to recover the workbook using Excel's built-in repair tools. If unsuccessful, restore from a backup copy or use third-party recovery tools to salvage data.

Understanding these common Excel error messages and their solutions, you can effectively troubleshoot and resolve issues that arise while working with Excel formulas and functions. Remember to double-check your formulas, data inputs, and references to prevent errors and ensure the accuracy of your calculations.

Additional Resources for Further Learning

Continuing to learn and expand your Excel skills is essential for maximizing productivity and efficiency. Here are some additional resources to further your learning and mastery of Excel:

1. Microsoft Excel Help Documentation:

Explore Excel's built-in help documentation for comprehensive information on features, functions, and capabilities. Use the Help menu or press F1 to access a wealth of tutorials, guides, and reference materials directly within Excel.

2. Online Courses and Tutorials:

Enroll in online courses and tutorials offered by platforms such as LinkedIn Learning, Udemy, and Coursera. These courses cover a wide range of topics, from beginner to advanced Excel skills, and are taught by experienced instructors.

3. Excel Books and Publications:

Invest in Excel books authored by experts in the field for in-depth coverage of advanced concepts, techniques, and best practices. Browse titles from publishers such as Wiley, O'Reilly, and Microsoft Press for comprehensive guides and reference materials.

4. Excel User Forums and Communities:

Join Excel user forums and communities such as MrExcel, Excel Forum, and Reddit's r/excel to connect with fellow users, ask questions, and share knowledge. Participating in discussions and forums can provide valuable insights, tips, and solutions from experienced users.

5. YouTube Channels and Video Tutorials:

Explore YouTube channels such as ExcelIsFun, MyOnlineTrainingHub, and Leila Gharani for video tutorials and demonstrations on Excel tips, tricks, and techniques. Video tutorials provide step-by-step guidance on using Excel features and functions effectively.

6. Microsoft Excel Blog and Newsletters:

Follow the Microsoft Excel Blog for updates, announcements, and tips on using Excel effectively. Subscribe to newsletters and email updates from Excel experts and influencers to stay informed about new features, best practices, and industry trends.

7. Excel Conferences and Events:

Attend Excel conferences, workshops, and events to network with professionals, learn from industry experts, and stay up-to-date with the latest developments in Excel. Look for conferences such as Excel Summit and Excelapalooza for opportunities to enhance your skills and connect with peers.

8. Excel Certification Programs:

Pursue Excel certification programs offered by organizations such as Microsoft and other accredited institutions. Excel certifications validate your proficiency in Excel and enhance your credibility in the job market.

9. Excel Webinars and Training Sessions:

Participate in Excel webinars and training sessions offered by software vendors, training providers, and industry associations. These sessions cover a wide range of topics, from basic Excel skills to advanced data analysis and visualization techniques.

10. Practice, Practice, Practice:

Finally, practice regularly to reinforce your Excel skills and apply what you've learned in real-world scenarios. Experiment with different formulas, functions, and techniques, and challenge yourself with complex tasks and projects to continually improve your proficiency in Excel.

By exploring these additional resources and actively engaging in continuous learning, you can enhance your Excel skills, increase your productivity, and unlock new possibilities for data analysis, reporting, and decision-making. Remember to approach learning with curiosity and persistence, and don't hesitate to seek help or guidance when needed.

Glossary of Excel Terms

Excel is a powerful spreadsheet software with its own set of terminology. Understanding these terms can help you navigate Excel more effectively. Here's a glossary of common Excel terms:

1. Workbook:
A file containing one or more worksheets.

2. Worksheet:
A single tab within a workbook where you enter and manipulate data.

3. Cell:

The intersection of a row and column in a worksheet, identified by a unique cell address (e.g., A1, B2).

4. Range:

A group of cells in a worksheet, identified by the starting and ending cell addresses (e.g., A1:B5).

5. Formula Bar:

The area above the worksheet grid where you enter or edit formulas and cell contents.

6. Formula:

An expression that performs calculations or manipulates data in a worksheet, beginning with an equal sign (=).

7. Function:

A built-in operation or calculation in Excel that performs a specific task, such as SUM, AVERAGE, or VLOOKUP.

8. Cell Reference:

A unique identifier for a cell in a worksheet, consisting of the column letter and row number (e.g., A1).

9. Relative Reference:

A cell reference that adjusts automatically when copied or moved to a new location in a worksheet.

10. Absolute Reference:

A cell reference that remains fixed when copied or moved to a new location in a worksheet, indicated by dollar signs ($).

11. Named Range:

A descriptive name assigned to a specific range of cells in a worksheet, making it easier to reference in formulas.

12. Pivot Table:

A data summarization tool in Excel that allows you to reorganize and analyze data from a worksheet.

13. Chart:

A visual representation of data in a worksheet, such as a bar chart, line chart, or pie chart.

14. Filter:

A tool in Excel that allows you to selectively display data based on specified criteria, hiding rows that do not meet the criteria.

15. Sort:

A tool in Excel that allows you to arrange data in ascending or descending order based on specified criteria.

16. Conditional Formatting:

A feature in Excel that allows you to format cells based on specified conditions or criteria, making it easier to identify trends and patterns in your data.

17. Data Validation:

A feature in Excel that allows you to control the type and format of data entered into cells, reducing errors and ensuring data integrity.

18. Macro:

A series of commands and actions recorded in Excel that can be replayed to automate repetitive tasks.

19. Ribbon:

The toolbar at the top of the Excel window contains tabs, groups, and commands for performing various tasks.

20. Quick Access Toolbar:

A customizable toolbar in Excel that allows you to add frequently used commands for quick access.

Understanding these Excel terms will help you navigate the software more confidently and make the most of its features and functionalities. Whether you're a beginner or an advanced user, familiarizing yourself with these terms is essential for Excel proficiency.

Conclusion

Excel is a versatile and powerful tool for data analysis, calculation, and visualization, with a wide range of features and functionalities to support various tasks and projects. Through this comprehensive guide, we have explored the essential functions, techniques, and best practices for maximizing productivity and efficiency in Excel.

From mastering basic arithmetic functions to harnessing the power of advanced techniques such as pivot tables, macros, and data analysis, you have gained valuable insights and skills to excel in Excel. By understanding the importance of data entry and management, implementing efficient strategies, and leveraging add-ins and plugins, you can streamline workflows, automate tasks, and unlock new possibilities for data-driven decision-making.

Furthermore, we have discussed common error messages and troubleshooting techniques to help you overcome challenges and maintain data integrity. Additionally, we have provided a glossary of Excel terms and curated a list of additional resources for further learning and exploration.

As you continue your journey with Excel, remember that practice, persistence, and continuous learning are key to mastering this powerful tool. Whether you're a student, professional, or enthusiast, Excel offers endless opportunities for analysis, reporting, and collaboration. Embrace its capabilities, experiment with different features, and stay curious as you uncover new ways to leverage Excel for your projects and endeavors.

With dedication and effort, you can become proficient in Excel and harness its full potential to achieve your goals and excel in your endeavors. Thank you for embarking on this journey with us, and we wish you success in your Excel endeavors!

Recap of Key Learnings

Throughout this guide, we've covered a wide range of topics and techniques to help you master Excel and become more proficient in using this powerful spreadsheet software. Here's a recap of the key learnings:

1. Essential Functions: Understand the fundamental arithmetic, statistical, and logical functions in Excel, such as SUM, AVERAGE, IF, and VLOOKUP, to perform basic calculations and data analysis.

2. Advanced Techniques: Explore advanced features like pivot tables, macros, and data analysis tools to analyze large datasets, automate repetitive tasks, and derive meaningful insights from your data.

3. Data Management: Learn best practices for data entry, validation, and manipulation to ensure accuracy, consistency, and integrity of your data.

4. Troubleshooting: Familiarize yourself with common error messages and solutions to troubleshoot issues effectively and prevent errors in your Excel workbooks.

5. Efficiency Strategies: Implement time-saving tips, keyboard shortcuts, and customization options to streamline your workflow and boost productivity in Excel.

6. Add-ins and Plugins: Discover additional tools and extensions, such as Power Query, Power Pivot, and third-party add-ins, to extend Excel's capabilities and enhance your data analysis and reporting.

7. Collaboration and Sharing: Explore features for collaboration and sharing, including sharing workbooks, co-authoring, and integrating with cloud storage services, to facilitate teamwork and communication among team members.

8. Continuous Learning: Take advantage of online courses, tutorials, forums, and other resources to continue learning and expanding your Excel skills, staying up-to-date with the latest developments and best practices.

Applying these key learnings, you can unlock the full potential of Excel and become more efficient, effective, and confident in your data analysis and reporting tasks. Whether you're a beginner or an experienced user, Excel offers endless opportunities for growth and innovation, empowering you to achieve your goals and excel in your endeavors. Keep practicing, exploring, and learning, and you'll soon become a master of Excel.

Future Trends in Excel

As technology continues to evolve, Excel is expected to adapt and incorporate new features and functionalities to meet the changing needs of users.

Here are some future trends we can expect to see in Excel:

1. Integration with Artificial Intelligence (AI): Excel may leverage AI technologies, such as machine learning algorithms, to provide intelligent insights, automate tasks, and assist users in data analysis and decision-making processes.

2. Enhanced Data Visualization: Excel may introduce advanced data visualization tools and techniques, including interactive dashboards, 3D charts, and augmented reality (AR) visualizations, to help users better understand and communicate insights from their data.

3. Cloud Collaboration and Real-time Updates: Excel may further enhance its cloud capabilities, allowing users to collaborate on workbooks in real-time, access data from anywhere, and receive automatic updates and notifications.

4. Natural Language Processing (NLP): Excel could integrate NLP capabilities, enabling users to interact with spreadsheets using natural language commands, queries, and voice inputs, making data analysis more intuitive and accessible.

5. Blockchain Integration: Excel may incorporate blockchain technology for secure and transparent data storage, validation, and sharing, enabling users to track and audit changes to their data with greater confidence and accountability.

6. Advanced Automation and Macros: Excel may introduce more advanced automation features and macro capabilities, allowing users to automate complex tasks, workflows, and business processes with ease.

7. Mobile Optimization: Excel may continue to improve its mobile experience, optimizing the interface and functionality for smartphones and tablets, and introducing new features specifically designed for mobile use cases.

8. Data Privacy and Security Enhancements: Excel may enhance its data privacy and security features, including encryption, access controls, and compliance certifications, to meet evolving regulatory requirements and protect sensitive information.

9. Enhanced Collaboration with Other Tools: Excel may strengthen its integration with other productivity tools and platforms, such as Microsoft Teams, Power BI, and SharePoint, to enable seamless collaboration and data exchange across the Microsoft ecosystem.

10. Customization and Personalization: Excel may offer more customization options and personalized experiences, allowing users to tailor the interface, formulas, and features to their specific preferences and workflows.

Embracing these future trends, Excel can continue to empower users with powerful tools and capabilities for data analysis, visualization, and collaboration, helping them achieve their goals and excel in their endeavors in the rapidly evolving digital landscape.

Continuing Your Excel Journey

Congratulations on completing this guide to mastering Excel! However, your journey with Excel doesn't end here.

The steps to continue your Excel journey and further enhance your skills:

1. NPractice Regularly: The more you use Excel, the more proficient you'll become. Practice regularly by working on projects, solving problems, and experimenting with new features and functions.

2. Explore Advanced Topics: Dive deeper into advanced topics such as Power Query, Power Pivot, macros, and VBA programming to unlock additional capabilities and automate complex tasks.

3. Stay Updated: Keep abreast of the latest updates, features, and trends in Excel by following Microsoft's announcements, attending webinars, and exploring online resources.

4. Join Excel Communities: Join online forums, communities, and social media groups dedicated to Excel, where you can ask questions, share tips, and learn from fellow enthusiasts and experts.

5. Take Online Courses: Enroll in online courses and tutorials on platforms like LinkedIn Learning, Udemy, and Coursera to continue expanding your Excel skills and knowledge.

6. Read Books and Publications: Explore books, eBooks, and publications on Excel authored by experts in the field to gain in-depth insights and practical guidance on advanced topics and techniques.

7. Experiment with Add-ins: Explore third-party add-ons and plugins to extend Excel's capabilities and enhance your productivity in areas such as data analysis, visualization, and automation.

8. Attend Workshops and Conferences: Attend workshops, conferences, and seminars on Excel to network with professionals, learn from industry experts, and stay up-to-date with the latest developments.

9. Teach Others: Share your knowledge and expertise with others by teaching Excel skills to colleagues, friends, or students, which can reinforce your own understanding and mastery of the software.

10. Set Goals: Set specific goals and objectives for your Excel journey, whether it's mastering a particular feature, completing a certification program, or solving a complex problem. Track your progress and celebrate your achievements along the way.

Excel is a journey, not a destination. Embrace the learning process, stay curious, and don't be afraid to explore new features and techniques. With dedication, practice, and a willingness to learn, you can continue to excel in Excel and leverage its full potential for your personal and professional growth.

www.ingramcontent.com/pod-product-compliance
Lightning Source LLC
LaVergne TN
LVHW051344050326
832903LV00031B/3728